Army Strong

My natural battle with cancer

Healing recipes
after the Gerson therapy

Copyright © 2013 by Shannon Sayers

All rights reserved.

This book is licensed for your personal enjoyment only. This book may not be re-sold or given away to other people. If you would like to share this book with another person, please purchase an additional copy for each recipient. If you're reading this book and did not purchase it, or it was not purchased for your use only, then please purchase your own copy. Thank you for respecting the hard work of this author.

*You never know how **strong** you are
until being **strong** is the **only** choice you have.*

Lord, make me an instrument of Thy peace;
where there is hatred, let me sow love;
where there is injury, pardon;
where there is doubt, faith;
where there is despair, hope;
where there is darkness, light;
and where there is sadness, joy.

O Divine Master,
grant that I may not so much seek to be consoled as to console;
to be understood, as to understand;
to be loved, as to love;
for it is in giving that we receive,
it is in pardoning that we are pardoned,
and it is in dying that we are born to eternal life.

Amen

St. Francis of Assisi - 13th century

My definition of Army Strong

A	R	M	Y	*	S	T	R	O	N	G
L	E	E	O		T	E	E	X	U	R
K	C	D	U		R	N	M	Y	T	O
A	O	I	T		E	A	I	G	R	W
L	V	T	H		N	C	S	E	I	T
I	E	A	F		G	I	S	N	T	H
N	R	T	U		T	T	I		I	
E	Y	E	L		H	Y	O		O	
						N			N	

Table of Contents

Flax Banana Oat Pancake...29
Chia pudding..31
Goji Granola...32
Coconut Raspberry Mango Slushy...34
Coconut Cocoa Banana Smoothie..35
Cocoa Blueberry Maca Smoothie..36
Coconut Blueberry Raspberry Muffins.......................................37
Pumpkin Muffins..39
Quinoa Avocado Muffins..40
Banana Coconut Chia bread..42
Delicious Veggie Wraps...43
Coconut Naan Flat Bread..44
My Green Alkaline Drink..46
My Energizer Juice..48
Rice Seaweed Wraps...49
Curry Coconut Lentil Soup..51
Coconut Curry Pumpkin Soup..53
Spicy Moroccan Stew...55
Cashew Potato Chowder...57
Quinoa Chili..59
Quinoa Pecan Burgers..61
Black Bean Sweet Potato Burgers..63
Amazing Beet Salad..65
Never Ending Salad..67
Kale Salad...69
Curried Chickpea Salad...70
Apple Cider Salad Dressing...71
Aioli Pine Nut Dip...72
Pistachio Pesto Sauce..73
Cilantro Dressing Marinade..74
Hemp Hummus..75
Vegan Veggie Dip..76
Red Quinoa Hemp Curry Bowl..77
Mexican Brown Rice Bowl..79
Spinach Pesto Quinoa Spaghetti..81
Organic Air Popped Popcorn..83
Brown Rice Walnut Cashew Meatballs......................................84
Sweet Potato Burrito's..86

Coconut Quinoa Delight..88
Brown Rice Noodle Pad Thai...89
Pesto Pizza...91
Cheesy Brussels Sprouts...92
Vegan Nut Cheese...93
Honey Mustard Kale Chips..95
Sweet Potato Mash..97
Coconut Dream Balls...98
Organic Peanut Butter Cookies..100
Almond Butter Maple Cookies...102
Best Cocoa Avocado Pudding...104
Yummy Coconut Butter..105
Yummy Protein bars..106

I would like to thank my dear friend Juliet for giving me a nudge to write this recipe book and to my son's girlfriend Carmen who helped plant the idea in my head.

Also to Robert G. Wright, Author of *"Killing cancer - not people"*, for his touching words for the back cover of my book.

On the day of my 40th birthday, I arrived in Ireland for an amazing trip with my mom, dad and daughter Krisdee. My parents had given me the trip as a birthday present, and we spent three unforgettable weeks exploring the land of our heritage. It was the start of what I hoped would be a memorable year ahead; I was excited about the milestone of turning 40. I had a good life in Canada with my husband and three children, and I was happy.

Little did I know that nine months later I would find a lump in my breast. It did turn into a memorable year, but for all the wrong reasons.

Two and a half months later, I had a lumpectomy, and then five days after that, I was sitting in my surgeon's office receiving the word that no-one wants to hear: CANCER.

The tumour was 8.5cm. I learned that for every centimeter of a tumour, there are one billion cancer cells. This means that I had 8.5 billion cancer cells inside my body!

Eleven days later I was at the hospital being wheeled down to the operating room for a double mastectomy and some lymph node removal. And so began my journey.

I have never had any conventional treatment. I learned how to treat cancer naturally and without drugs from my mom (who had also battled breast cancer) and from reading many, many books. Through my learning, I have taken control of my own health.

My story is told in my mom's alternative therapy book, written by my friend Juliet Sullivan. It is entitled "All Shook Up" and I would highly recommend it for anyone that has just been diagnosed and is considering natural therapy. all-shook-up.com.

My mom has helped many cancer patients over the past 15 years; it is her passion. Her message is about opening your mind to other ways, including natural therapies and "changing the terrain of your body".

I am forever grateful for all her knowledge, which she has passed on to me, because without it, my story could have been a very different one.

After my surgery, I dove into the Gerson Therapy, which my mother did over 15 years ago. It was the cleanest eating I have ever done in my life! It consisted of 13 organic juices and 5 organic coffee enemas every day. I also overcame my fear of needles, as I learned how to inject myself with B-12/crude liver shots on a daily basis! It was tough, but through it I learned about the true meaning of clean eating. I followed it for a few months, and then decided to modify it to suit my needs. To this day, I use a lot of what I learned in that time for my own modified version of clean eating. I still make a green drink every day and twice a week I enjoy a delicious carrot and apple juice.

I have created my own cleaner eating recipes for my family and myself – although not as strict as The Gerson.

There is a lot of confusion about what to eat and what not to eat when battling cancer. At one point before I had the double mastectomy, I remember being so overwhelmed by the differing opinions, that I was hardly eating anything. That was hard for me, because I have a healthy appetite. These days, that healthy appetite is nourished by good, clean, healthy food. And I feel great.

This is not your ordinary cook book, and it is not full of goodies, though it does have a few – healthy – treats. These recipes have been modified to my own needs, through my own research, trial and error, and what I believe has worked for me.

I want to share these recipes with anyone who is looking for cleaner living and prevention; this is now my passion, as I follow in my mother's footsteps...

Kris Carr is a New York Times best-selling author, wellness activist and cancer thriver. Below is an extract from one of her blogs, reproduced with her kind permission.

Your gut holds trillions of bacteria that help process your food, produce nutrients, and fight disease. There are ten times more bacteria in your gut than cells in your entire body! Since what you eat, drink and think affects the environment in your gut, your daily choices play a critical role in whether those trillion plus bacteria help or hinder your well-being.

Your gut guides your overall well-being. By supporting this mighty system, you'll see chronic health issues (like fatigue, fogginess, colds, aches and pains) diminish, and you'll feel abundant energy return.

Feed your body plant-based, nutrient foods.

60-70 percent of your immune system lives in your gut.

It's all about balance when it comes to gut health. When your gut is in tip-top shape, about 80-85 percent of bacteria are good guys and 15-20 percent are bad guys. You feel great, your body is strong and nimble, you rarely get sick, your energy is consistent, but when the harmful bacteria stage a revolt, all hell breaks loose. They totally gum up the works and cause painful problems like inflammation and infection, which can then lead to health issues such as constipation, candida, allergies, arthritis, headaches, depression, autoimmune diseases and more.

Take a probiotic supplement to help keep the bad guys under control.

Lesson refined sugar and processed foods, as you are giving bad bacteria an all-you-can-eat buffet.

Stay hydrated.

Lessen stress - there is a connection between your brain and your gut.

Taken from Kris Karr's blog: `kriscarr.com/blog/how-to-improve-your-gut-health/`

Here are some of my favorite books that helped me in so many ways:

"Healing The Gerson way",
by Charlotte Gerson with Beata Bishop

"Killing cancer - not people",
by Robert G. Wright.

"The China study",
by Dr. T. Colin Campbell.

"The Rave diet, healing cancer from the inside out",
by Mike Anderson.

"The Enzyme factor",
by Hiromi Shinya MD

"The Blood sugar solution cookbook",
by Mark Hyman, MD

"Knowledge is the power to control your destiny."

A note about my recipes:

Shopping for the right ingredients is hugely important. When I am shopping, I buy only organic. I also like to support local farmers and businesses where possible.

I always read labels to make sure nothing is genetically modified. I only buy organic nuts and seeds, due to the carcinogenic sprays. When buying frozen berries, ensure that they are organic. DDT (one of the most dangerous pesticides) has been found in non-organic frozen berries.

A note about lifestyle:

I really believe in eating a 70-80% plant based, alkalizing diet, with a 20-30% acidic (but healthy) balance. For more information on acid/alkaline foods, Google the acid/alkaline foods list. I have heard many stories about women who have claimed not to experience menopause symptoms due to the fact that they are eating a predominantly plant based diet. That is because this way of eating is easier on your hormones. One of the women I have been following is Marilu Henner. You can find more information about her online.

Exercise is crucial on a regular basis to keep your lymphatic system clean. Aim for 4 to 5 days per week if you can. Break a sweat for at least 20 minutes!

A note about products:

I mention various utensils, equipment and products in the book. Below I have detailed where you can find more information on these products I would highly recommend.

Norwalk Juicer: `nwjcal.com`

Champion Juicer: `championjuicer.com`

Vitamix: `vitamix.com` or 1-800-848-2649 Use this reference code ***06-008581*** for FREE standard shipping and handling which is a $35CN/$25US value. (The company also sells refurbished machines.)

Vitamix® is a registered trademark of Vita-Mix Corporation.

Borner V slicer: `swissmar.com` (This amazing chopper does all the chopping for you!)

Flax Banana Oat Pancake
SERVINGS 2

"When something bad happens you have three choices you can either let it define you, let it destroy you, or you can let it strengthen you." ~Unknown

- 3/4 cup organic rolled oats (gluten free Bob's red mill)
- 1/4 cup gluten free all-purpose flour (gluten free Bob's red mill)
- 1/2 tsp baking powder (non-aluminum)
- 1/2 tsp baking soda (Bob's red mill)
- 1/2 tsp arrowroot starch flour (Bob's red mill)
- 1/2 cup unsweetened vanilla almond milk
- 1/4 piece of banana
- 1/4 cup fresh blueberries
- 1/4 cup fresh raspberries
- 1 tbsp golden brown ground flax mix with 3 tbsp water = 1 egg (egg replacer)
- 1/2 tsp virgin coconut oil
- 1 tbsp Udo's oil
- 1 tbsp hemp seeds (found at a health food store)
- Sprinkle unsweetened shredded coconut

Combine ground flax with 3 tbsp water and put on medium heat and stir well till it thickens about 3- 4 minutes. (Let cool a bit.)

Put all ingredients into the Vitamix® blender and blend till smooth. Add banana and flax mixture last and blend for a few seconds.

On medium heat add coconut oil to frying pan and pour batter onto pan.

Cook a few minutes on both sides till golden brown.

These pancakes take a little longer than the usual (with a knife check in the middle of pancake.)

Drizzle "grade 3" maple syrup, Udo's oil or coconut butter on top.

Sprinkle hemp seeds and shredded coconut all over.

Top with blueberries and raspberries.

I grind a 1/2 cup of golden brown flax seeds and store them in the freezer, that way you'll always have them on hand.

*Unsweetened almond milk contains no carrageenan. Scientists have raised serious concerns about the safety of carrageenan in food, based on laboratory animal studies showing gastrointestinal inflammation, ulcerations and colitis-like disease in animals given food-grade carrageenan in their drinking water or diet.

*Raspberries and blueberries are cancer fighting super foods. They are loaded with fiber, minerals and antioxidants that fight cancer and other diseases.

Chia pudding
SERVINGS 4

"All disease begins in the gut." ~Hippocrates, the father of modern medicine.

- **2/3 cup chia seeds (found at a health food store)**
- **1 tsp. cinnamon**
- **2 cups true almond unsweetened vanilla**
- **1/2 tsp. organic vanilla extract**
- **2 tbsp. "grade 3" maple syrup**
- **2 tbsp. unsweetened coconut flakes**
- **4 pitted unsulfured dates chopped finely or a few raisins**

Put chia seeds, almond milk, coconut, dates and vanilla in a 1-quart glass jar with a lid. Tighten the lid and shake well to thoroughly combine. Refrigerate overnight. When ready to serve, stir well. Top with fresh fruit.

Chia seeds soaked overnight turn into a pudding, similar to tapioca.

*Almond unsweetened vanilla milk contains only 30 calories per cup and is loaded with vitamins, minerals and antioxidants.

Goji Granola
4-5 SERVINGS

"Every life experience that occurs is there for the benefit of your awakening if you choose to see it... Everything is happening to choose you, to awaken to your 'true self.'"
~Unknown

- **2 cups of gluten free oats (Bob's red mill)**
- **1/2 cup of slivered almonds**
- **1/4 cup pumpkin seeds**
- **1/2 cup goji berries**
- **1/2 cup hemp seeds (found at a health food store)**
- **3 tsp cinnamon**
- **1 tsp organic vanilla extract**
- **3 tbsp virgin coconut oil (melted)**
- **1/4 cup freshly squeezed orange or 1/4 cup mangosteen juice**
- **1/3 cup "grade 3" maple syrup**
- **1 tbsp coconut flour**
- **1/2 cup unsweetened shredded coconut**

Preheat oven to 350.

Melt coconut oil and set aside.

Using a hand held citrus juicer with a measuring cup, squeeze the orange to make the fresh juice.

Combine oat (not quick oats) cinnamon, vanilla, orange juice, maple syrup, coconut flour in a bowl, pour in coconut oil and toss well.

Place parchment paper on cookie sheet and spread out granola mixture.

Set timer for 20 minutes. Once the timer beeps, toss really well. Set timer again for another 20 min.

Take out and let cool. Mix in hemp, goji, pumpkin seeds, shredded coconut, and chopped almonds. Toss well.

Store granola in a glass container in the pantry.

I enjoy it for breakfast with fresh organic blueberries and unsweetened vanilla almond milk.

"This granola goes very fast in my household make sure to double the recipe!"

*Goji berries are rich in antioxidants, particularly beta carotene. They are great when it comes to protecting the liver and kidneys.

Coconut Raspberry Mango Slushy
SERVINGS 2

"To make the right choices in life, you have to get in touch with your soul. To do this, you need to experience solitude, which most people are afraid of, because in the silence you hear the truth and know the solutions." ~Deepak Chopra

1 cup "vita kosher" coconut water (found at a health food store)

1/4 cup unsweetened organic coconut milk (BPA free) "Natural value"

1 tbsp fresh lime juice

1 tsp honey

3 medjool pitted dates (unsulfured)

1/2 cup fresh raspberries

1/4 cup frozen mango's

1 kiwi peeled

1 cup coconut ice cubes

Pour coconut water into ice cube trays and freeze overnight.

Put coconut water and dates into the Vitamix blender and blend till dates are pureed. Put remaining ingredients into blender and blend till slushy.

You may add more coconut ice cubes if needed.

I love my Vitamix® blender, I use it every day!

*Coconut water has an alkalizing effect on the body, helping counteract or balance the effects of acidifying foods which are so common in our diets.

Coconut Cocoa Banana Smoothie
SERVINGS 2

"You cannot always wait for the perfect time; sometimes you must dare to jump." ~Unknown

1 cup organic unsweetened canned coconut milk (BPA-free) "Natural value"

1 tbsp raw organic unsweetened cocoa powder (found at a health food store)

1 tbsp hemp seeds (found at a health food store)

1 tbsp chia seeds grind into powder using the Vitamix blender (dry container)

1 tbsp nut butter (your choice)

1 tbsp "grade 3" maple syrup

1/2 banana

1 cup coconut ice cubes

Put all ingredients into the Vitamix® blender and blend till creamy and smooth.

*Organic raw cocoa powder is at the top of the antioxidant list with almost four times the amount of antioxidant as goji berries.

Cocoa Blueberry Maca Smoothie
Servings 2

"If YOU realized how POWERFUL your THOUGHTS were, you would never think a NEGATIVE thought again."
~Peace Pilgrim

1 1/2 cups canned organic unsweetened coconut milk (BPA free) "Natural value"

2 tsp raw honey

2 tbsp unsweetened cocoa powder

2 tbsp maca powder

1/4 cup frozen blueberries

1/2 of a banana

Handful of coconut ice cubes

Put all ingredients into the Vitamix® blender and blend until creamy.

*Maca is known as an adaptogen, a plant that is able to balance hormone levels and revitalize the whole body.

It also enhances energy and is great for stress.

Coconut Blueberry Raspberry Muffins
SERVINGS 12 MUFFINS

"If you can't pronounce it, DON'T EAT IT."
~Common Sense

- 1/2 cup coconut flour
- 1/2 cup amaranth powder (Bob's red mill)
- 1 cup gluten free all-purpose flour (Bob's red mill)
- 1 tsp baking powder (non-aluminum)
- 1/4 cup unsweetened shredded coconut flakes
- 1/2 tsp Himalayan sea salt
- 1 tbsp golden brown flax seeds (grinded)
- 1 cup fresh blueberries
- 1 cup fresh raspberries
- 1/3 cup raw organic honey
- 9 pitted unsulfured dates
- 2 tbsp apple cider vinegar + 2 tsp baking soda
- 2 tsp vanilla extract
- 1/2 cup organic unsweetened canned coconut milk (BPA-free) "Natural value"
- 1 tbsp coconut oil (melted)
- 1/2 cup apple sauce = 1 apple (home-made see recipe below)

Preheat oven to 330 degrees.

Boil water and add in a whole apple cored cut into pieces, boil for 4 min. Drain hot water and add some cold water to cool.

Drain water once apples have cooled.

Coat the berries in some gluten free flour. Set aside.

Mix all the flours and baking powder, shredded coconut, sea salt together.

Pour coconut oil, coconut milk, cooked apple, honey, vanilla and dates into the Vitamix® blender and blend till creamy.

Mix apple cider vinegar and baking soda in a cup, then stir into blended ingredients.

Pour liquid into dry mix and stir well.

Fold in berries.

Put into muffin pan and bake for 25-30 minutes.

Let cool and put in glass container and store in refrigerator.

*Blueberries are a powerful antioxidant which helps the immune system and helps protect cells by stabilizing free radicals and can prevent some of the damage they cause.

Pumpkin Muffins
SERVINGS 12

"Your mind is a garden, your thoughts are the seeds, you can grow flowers or you can grow weeds." ~Unknown

1 cup sorghum flour

1/3 cup chia seeds grind into powder using the Vitamix blender® (dry container)

1 cup oats "not quick oats" grind into powder using Vitamix blender (dry container)

1 tsp baking soda (non-aluminum)

1/2 cup pecans chopped

4 pitted unsulfured dates

1 tsp nutmeg

2 tsp cinnamon

1 15 oz can of pumpkin

1/4 cup unsweetened vanilla almond milk

1/4 cup virgin coconut oil (melted)

1/4 cup raw honey

1/2 cup apple sauce (homemade)

Blend almond milk, pumpkin, honey, coconut oil, dates into Vitamix® blender until creamy.

In a large bowl combine sorghum, ground up oats and chia seeds, baking soda, pecans.

Add blended pumpkin mixture to flour mixture and blend well.

Put in muffin pan and bake at 350 for 30 minutes.

*Pumpkin is rich in vital antioxidants, vitamin, minerals and fiber.

Quinoa Avocado Muffins
Servings 12

"May flowers always line your path and sunshine light your day. May songbirds serenade you every step along the way. May a rainbow run beside you in a sky that's always blue? And may happiness fill your heart each day your whole life through." ~Traditional Irish Blessing

- 1 cup sweet white sorghum gluten free flour (Bob's red mill)
- 1/2 cup amaranth gluten free flour (Bob's red mill)
- 1/2 cup of organic raw unsweetened cocoa powder
- 1 tsp baking soda (Bob's red mill)
- 1 tsp baking powder (non-aluminum)
- 1/2 cup unsweetened shredded coconut (optional)
- 1/2 cup unsweetened vanilla almond milk
- 1 cup cooked quinoa
- 1/2 cup of apple sauce (homemade = 1 small apple)
- 1 large avocado (mashed)
- 1 ripe banana (mashed)
- 1/3 cup "grade 3" maple syrup
- 5 unsulfured pitted medjool dates (they are a lot bigger than regular dates)
- 2 tbsp virgin coconut oil
- 1 tbsp golden brown ground flax mix with 3 tbsp water (egg replacer)

Preheat oven to 350.

Cut apple in pieces and take out core. Add apples to boiling water and cook for 3-4 minutes. Drain and let cool.

Combine freshly ground flax with water and put on medium heat and stir well till it thickens about 3 minutes. (Let cool a bit.)

Put all dry ingredients into a large bowl and mix together.

Pour almond milk, maple syrup, dates, flax mixture, avocado and apples into the Vitamix® blender and blend on high till all the dates are blended well.

In a separate bowl mash the banana with a masher and then add in cooked quinoa. (I do not blend bananas in the blender for this recipe, as they can make the muffins to gummy.)

Pour blended ingredients in with the banana mixture using a spatula to scrape any liquid from the sides and mix well.

Add dry ingredients to the wet and mix all together. (Do not over mix.)

Spoon the mixture into muffin pan.

Bake for 30 minutes.

Let cool when done and store in a glass Tupperware in the pantry.

*Bananas are an excellent source of potassium and magnesium. The high potassium content promotes bone health to.

They also have a high content of antioxidant phenolic compounds.

It's a great food to be eaten right after a workout.

Banana Coconut Chia bread
Servings 12

"YOU ARE EXACTLY where YOU ARE SUPPOSED to be."
~Unknown

3 very ripe organic bananas

1/2 cup raw organic honey

3 tbsp virgin coconut oil (melted)

1 tbsp organic vanilla

1 1/2 cups gluten free all-purpose baking flour (Bob's Red Mill)

1/4 cup chia seeds grind into a powder using the Vitamix® blender (dry container)

1/4 unsweetened shredded coconut

1/4 tsp Himalayan sea salt

1 tsp cinnamon

1 1/2 tsp baking soda (Bob's red mill)

1 1/2 tsp arrowroot starch flour (Bob's red mill), mix well with 2 tbsp of warm water

3/4 cup chopped pecans

Preheat oven to 350. Mash the bananas and mix honey, oil, vanilla and arrowroot mixture.

In another bowl stir together flour, baking soda, shredded coconut, salt, chia seeds, cinnamon and nuts.

Add wet mixture to dry and stir well.

Put in oiled loaf pan, bake for 35-40 min (check with a fork.)

*Chia actually got its name from the Mayan word for "strength."

The benefits of chia include fiber, omega fatty acids, calcium, and antioxidants. And even protein.

Delicious Veggie Wraps
Servings 2

"Physical strength measured by what we can carry; Spiritual is by what we can bear." ~Unknown

- **2 gluten free wraps (or my homemade naan bread)**
- **1 cup broccoli florets washed**
- **1/2 cup onions sliced thinly**
- **1/4 cup avocado sliced**
- **1/4 cup red cabbage shredded**
- **1/4 cup carrots shredded**
- **1/2 cup spinach washed**
- **2 tbsp roasted unsalted sunflower seeds**
- **1 tbsp natural barbecue sauce "Amazing dad's bbq sauce" (gluten free)**
- **2 tsp vegenaise**

Sauté onions and barbeque sauce on medium heat. Stir till they are caramelized.

Place your wrap on a plate and spread vegenaise all over.

Top with onions, avocado, cabbage, carrots, spinach, broccoli and sprinkle sunflower seeds on top.

Fold over to make a wrap like taco and enjoy!

*Red cabbage is a good source of phytonutrients that help to detoxify pollutants and other carcinogens that most people are exposed to on a daily basis. People who consume high quantities of cruciferous vegetables have been shown to have lower risk of certain types of cancer. Red cabbage is also a good source of indoles, compounds that may reduce the risk of breast cancer by altering estrogen metabolism.

Coconut Naan Flat Bread

Servings 4-7 (depending on your size preference)

"There is not ONE path. There is not even the RIGHT path. There is only YOUR path... and you know it's yours by how it feels to you." ~Sue Krebs

- 2 1/4 cups gluten free all-purpose flour (Bob's red mill)
- 1/4 cup organic coconut flour
- 2 tbsp psyllium husk powder
- 3 tbsp coconut oil
- 2 tbsp arrowroot starch/flour (Bob's red mill)
- 1 tbsp chia seeds grind into a powder using the Vitamix blender® (dry container)
- 1 tsp baking powder (non-aluminum)
- 1 tbsp apple cider vinegar + 1 tsp baking soda (mix in a cup)
- 1/2 tsp onion powder
- 1/2 tsp garlic powder
- 1/2 tsp Himalayan sea salt
- 2 tbsp "grade 3" maple syrup
- 1 cup of warmed vegetable broth "kitchen basic" no salt added (found at a health food store) or water

In a large mixing bowl add the dry ingredients and mix well.

In a saucepan warm broth, coconut oil and maple syrup. (Do not boil.) Add hot liquid to dry mix. Add in apple cider vinegar mixture and mix until almost absorbed. Using your hands mix well and form into 2 large balls.

The dough should feel like play dough.

Place all but one of the dough balls back into the bowl and cover with a clean dish towel until you're ready to roll them.

Place a big sheet of parchment paper on the counter and sprinkle a bit of gluten free all-purpose mix on the parchment paper as well as on top of dough before you roll each of the balls.

Form into a good size circular shape using a dough roller. Cut around with a sharp knife to form a circle. Add back the extra pieces of dough each time you form a new piece. Make sure to use a nice chunk of dough each time you begin to roll it out. If there is a slight tear in the rolled out dough, add a little piece of dough over top and press down using your fingers.

On medium heat drizzle a little grapeseed oil in frying pan and put the flat piece of dough into the pan.

Cook for 2-3 minutes on each side.

Put cooked flat bread on a covered plate to stay warm. I like to roll the dough, while another is cooking. (Be sure to time each one so they don't burn.)

You can make this flat bread into a bigger wrap by spreading it further out.

Serve them warm with hummus or my soups and veggie wraps.

*When buying gluten free products in a grocery store, make sure to read the ingredients. You want to see clean ingredients. Avoid canola oil, refined sugars, guar gum and Xanthan gum.

*Psyllium has been shown to be quite effective in lowering LDL (bad) cholesterol and studies have reported it may help enhance the sensation of fullness and reduce hunger cravings which will aid in weight loss.

My Green Alkaline Drink
Serving 1

"To my children, if I had to choose between loving you and breathing... I would use my last breath to tell you... I Love You!" ~Unknown

- 1/2 cup of organic pineapple coconut juice
- 1/2 cup alkaline water
- 1 tbsp flax or Udo's oil
- 1/4 cup blueberries
- 1/4 piece of a banana
- 3 dandelion greens
- 2 leaves of collard greens
- 1 cup of washed spinach (big handful)
- 2 scoops of a vegan Isagenix harvest berry protein powder (plant-based)

Put all ingredients into the Vitamix® blender and blend till all your greens are blended and smooth.

I really enjoy this as my lunch some days, it's really filling!

If I have eaten lunch, I make this around 3 pm (my snack) and just omit the 2 scoops of vegan protein powder.

*When you drink it right out of the blender, it instantly goes straight to the GI tract which floods the body with all these much needed nutrients, giving you lots of energy.

For information on this delicious pea and hemp vegan-based (gluten free) protein powder, go to:

```
cleanbodyleanbody.isagenix.com
```

They also have a wonderful full body cleansing system I love to do frequently.

* Dandelion is a great detoxifier and can reduce the risk of cancer!

It is high in antioxidants such as vitamin c and luteolin which reduce the free radicals in the body.

My Energizer Juice
Servings 1

"I am healed, whole and healthy!" ~Unknown

- 1 beet peeled and sliced in half
- 4 large carrots washed (use a veggie scrubber)
- 1 cup of red cabbage washed and cut into a couple pieces.
- 1 apple cored washed and cut into pieces
- 2 tbsp fresh ginger peeled
- 1/2 a lemon squeezed (add to juice)

Make sure to have a good juicer, I use a champion juicer along with a hydraulic press.

*Ginger helps strengthens your immunity which is great for colds and flu prevention. It reduces pain and inflammation.

It may be a powerful weapon in the treatment of ovarian cancer.

Studies have found that ginger powder induced cell death.

Juicers: There are plenty of models on the market. The simplest and cheapest is called the 'centrifugal' type and produces deficient, enzyme-poor juice and cannot be used for healing.

The best two-process juicer is the Norwalk Hydraulic press juicer.

Rice Seaweed Wraps
SERVINGS 4

"Keep CALM and EAT PLANT STRONG." ~Unknown

8 rice paper (wrappers)

1 small package of toasted seaweed snacks (canola oil free)

2 avocado sliced

1 cup bean sprouts

4 carrots shredded

1 cup cilantro chopped

1 green pepper sliced finely

4 green onions sliced diagonally

2 cups arugula

1/2 cup roasted unsalted peanuts chopped finely or cashews

1/4 cup sesame seeds

Sauce:

2 tbsp almond butter

1 tbsp Bragg's seasoning

2 tbsp rice vinegar

2 tbsp raw honey

1 freshly squeezed Lime

1 tbsp fresh ginger grated

1/4 cup sesame oil

Blend sauce ingredients in magic bullet blender till ginger is fully chopped and creamy.

Take all ingredients and place them on a large cooking area. (Ready to create your wrap)

Soak each sheet for 30 seconds in water.

For each wrap I use 2 rice papers to create a bigger circle. They are much easier to roll and wrap.

Put sheet flat on counter and top each one with sea weed and all the ingredients.

Drizzle sauce on top.

Fold over bottom of sheet, then fold in both sides and roll it into a wrap,

Repeat method.

My kids like cooked pieces of organic chicken or wild salmon inside the wraps

*Dried seaweed is rich in Iodine, Iron, calcium, vitamin k, folate, phytonutrients, carotenoids and magnesium.

It also is a good source of amino acids

*I take liquid sea veggies from a company called Sealogica, Which is a raw whole food blend of 7 wild-harvested sea vegetables, harvested from the coldest water from around the world. For more information contact me through my Hotmail, Shea82@hotmail.com

Curry Coconut Lentil Soup
SERVINGS 5

"As you become more fearless, fear itself loses a grip on you."
~Rev Michael Beckwith

2 cups of lentils (soaked for 1 hour)

3 cups of vegetable broth "kitchen basic" no salt added (found at a health food store)

1 can of unsweetened canned organic coconut milk (BPA free) "Natural value"

1 large onion chopped

2 tbsp freshly grated ginger

4 garlic cloves minced

2 large carrots chopped

2 sweet potatoes diced

3 cups of kale stemmed

1 tsp cinnamon

1 1/2 tsp curry powder

1 tsp turmeric

1/2 tsp cardamom

1/4 tsp nutmeg

1 tsp Himalayan sea salt

3 tbsp fresh lime juice

2 tbsp virgin coconut oil

1/2 cup unsweetened shredded coconut

1/2 cup chopped cilantro

Fresh ground pepper

In a large pot add broth, lentils and sweet potato. Bring to a boil, put lid on and turn down to a simmer. Cook for about 20 minutes.

Sauté on med heat onions, carrots and garlic with coconut oil till carrots are slightly done. Reduce to low. Add in the rest of the spices and lime juice, stir well for 1 minute.

Once the lentils are cooked, add the sautéed onion mixture and stir.

Keep lentils on low heat and add in coconut milk, kale and cilantro. Let simmer for 10 minutes.

When ready to serve add in shredded coconut and ground pepper to taste.

*Lentils have beneficial nutrients like fiber, protein, minerals and vitamins. They are low in calories and are great for stabilizing blood sugar levels.

Coconut Curry Pumpkin Soup
Servings 5

"Never give up hope...Never stop living..." ~Shannon Sayers

- 1 15oz canned (BPA free) organic pumpkin
- 4 red potatoes cubed
- 1 large white onion
- 1 leek chopped (use up to one inch above the white part)
- 2 large carrots diagonally sliced
- 3 cups cauliflower chopped into small florets
- 4 garlic cloves
- 1 tbsp fresh ginger grated
- 3 cups vegetable broth "kitchen basic" no salt added (found at a health food store)
- 1 cup of organic unsweetened coconut milk (BPA free) "Natural value"
- 2 tbsp "grade 3" maple syrup
- 3 tbsp sprouted chickpea miso (found at a health food store)
- 1 tbsp fresh lemon juice
- 1 tbsp virgin coconut oil
- 3 tsp curry powder
- 1/2 tsp nutmeg
- 1/2 tsp Himalayan sea salt
- 2 tbsp fresh parsley chopped

Heat coconut oil in a large pot over medium-high heat.

Add in onions, carrots, leek, garlic, ginger, sea salt, nutmeg and curry powder.

Sauté for 3 minutes. Add in vegetable broth, pumpkin, chick pea miso, potatoes, and lemon juice.

Stir well and bring to boil for 5 minutes.

Reduce heat to low and cover.

Let simmer for 1 hour

Pour 1/4 of the soup into the Vitamix® blender and blend till creamy. Add back into pot and stir well.

Before serving add in maple syrup and coconut milk, sea salt and stir well.

Garnish with parsley and fresh ground pepper to taste.

*Leeks like garlic and onions belong to the same family. They contain many of the same beneficial compounds found in these health-promoting vegetables.

*I ate leeks every day on the Gerson therapy.

Spicy Moroccan Stew
SERVINGS 6

"If you realized how powerful your thoughts where, you would never think a negative thought again." ~Peace Pilgrim

3 cups of vegetable broth "kitchen basic" no salt added (found at a health food store)

1 can unsweetened organic coconut milk (BPA free) "Natural value"

1 large onion chopped

5 garlic cloves minced

2 sweet potatoes peeled and chopped into cubes

2 yams peeled and chopped into cubes

1 green pepper chopped

3 stalks of celery chopped

3 carrots chopped

1 cup zucchini chopped

1/2 cup pitted green olives sliced in half

2 cups kale stemmed and chopped

1 19 oz. can of tomatoes, drained

2 cups of chickpeas (soaked overnight and cooked)

1 cup lentils (soaked for 1 hour)

1 tbsp fresh ginger grated

1 tbsp chili powder

2 tsp curry powder

1 tsp cumin

1 tsp cinnamon

1 tsp coriander

1 tsp turmeric

1/2 tsp nutmeg

1/2 tsp Himalayan sea salt

- **1/4 cup cilantro chopped**
- **2 tbsp lime juice**
- **1 tbsp natural peanut butter or almond**
- **1 tbsp virgin coconut oil**

Heat coconut oil in a large soup pot over medium high heat, add coconut oil, onions, celery, green pepper, carrots, zucchini and garlic and sauté for 5 minutes stirring constantly.

Add broth, spices, coconut milk and stir well. Add sweet potatoes, yams, lime juice, lentils except the peanut butter and cilantro.

Stir well and bring to a rapid boil for a few minutes.

Add in peanut butter, cilantro, kale and olives and stir well. Reduce heat to very low temperature and cover with lid.

Let simmer for 1 hour.

Garnish with cilantro and fresh ground pepper to taste.

*Turmeric is the king of all spices when it comes to dealing with cancer diseases. It contains the powerful polyphenol that has been clinically proven to retard the growth of cancer cells and not pose a threat to healthy cells in the body.

*For almost 3 years I have been taking 8 turmeric pills every day through a company called, Enagic.

I also purchased an alkaline- antioxidant water machine which I drink my 8-10 glasses of water a day. My parents purchased the shower head for me as a gift. It removes all chlorine.

When I did the Gerson therapy, I was not allowed to shower or bathe with chlorinated water.

If interested in this amazing antioxidant water machine or the turmeric pills from Japan, contact me through my Hotmail, Shea82@hotmail.com

Cashew Potato Chowder
SERVINGS 5

"To keep the body in good health is a duty, otherwise we shall not be able to keep our mind strong and clear." ~Buddha

3 cups potatoes peeled and cubed

2 cups sweet potatoes peeled and cubed

4 cloves garlic minced

1 large onion diced

1 leek (white and light green part only) chopped

3 large carrots diced

1 red pepper chopped

1 cup celery chopped

1 cup frozen corn niblets (non-GMO)

4 cups vegetable broth "kitchen basic" no salt added (found at a health food store)

1 cup water

3/4 cup organic white wine (alcohol will be cooked off)

1/2 cup cashews (soaked for 1 hour)

2 tbsp virgin coconut oil

1/4 cup nutritional yeast

1 tbsp chick pea miso (found at a health food store)

1 tbsp Bragg's seasoning

1 tbsp dried parsley

1 tbsp dried dill

1/4 chopped fresh dill

1/4 tsp cayenne pepper

1/2 tsp Himalayan sea salt

Freshly ground pepper

Soak cashews for 1 hour. Drain when ready to use.

In a sauce pan on medium heat add coconut oil, onions, garlic, red pepper, leeks, wine and sea salt. Stir constantly for 5 minutes. Set aside.

In a large pot add veggie broth and water, bring to a boil and add in carrots, corn, potatoes, miso, parsley, dried dill, cayenne pepper and Bragg's, boil for 5 minutes. Reduce heat to low and cover with lid, simmer for 45 minutes.

Take 2 cups of the cooked potato mixture, cashews, water, and nutritional yeast. Pour into the Vitamix® blender and blend until smooth.

Add blended liquid to soup pot, stir and season with cayenne pepper, fresh dill, sea salt and pepper to taste.

*Chick pea miso is soya free, organic and kosher certified. It is rich in nutrients, due in part to its fermentation process. It contains vitamins B2, E, K, calcium, iron, potassium, choline and lecithin. Miso is also a great source of live lactobacilli, which enhances your body's ability to extract nutrients from food. It is high in dietary fiber and protein.

Some health food stores do not carry this product. To find a store located near you, check out their web-site:

                gallowaysfoods.com

Quinoa Chili
SERVINGS 4-5

"No matter how good or bad you think life is, wake up each day and be THANKFUL FOR LIFE...

Someone somewhere else is fighting to survive." ~Unknown

3 cups cooked organic quinoa

1 1/2 cups black beans soaked overnight or canned (BPA free) black beans

1 1/2 cups kidney beans soaked overnight or canned (BPA free) kidney beans

1 cup navy beans soaked overnight or canned (BPA free) navy beans

16 oz can organic tomato paste (BPA free)

1 jar and 1/2 of organic (olive oil) spaghetti sauce

1 tbsp apple cider vinegar

6 organic garlic cloves chopped

1 big organic onion chopped

4 stalks of organic celery chopped

3 large organic carrots chopped diagonally

1 organic green pepper chopped

1 cup organic cilantro chopped

1/2 tsp smoked paprika

2 tsp cumin

3 tbsp chili powder

1/2 tsp chipotle chili pepper spice

3 tbsp black strap molasses (unsulfured)

1 tbsp virgin coconut oil or grapeseed oil

3 tbsp nutritional yeast

1 bag of healthy taco chips (canola oil free)

3 avocado chopped

Drain and rinse beans. Add beans in a large pot with 2 times the amount of water to beans. Boil for 4 minutes, then cover with a lid and simmer on low for 1 1/2 hours.

Before cooking quinoa, rinse in a metal strainer to make sure the resin-like coating is all off.

On medium heat, sauté all the veggies with coconut oil for 4-5 minutes. Add all the spices, apple cider vinegar, tomato paste and 1/2 cup of cilantro, add in molasses and stir well for 4-5 minutes.

Put cooked beans, quinoa, tomato sauce, nutritional yeast in a large pot.

Add in mixture from frying pan, mix well. Cover and simmer on low for an hour.

Top with fresh cilantro.

Serve it with taco chips around your plate and chopped avocado.

My family enjoys it with cooked organic ground turkey and a little organic sour cream.

You may use canned beans, but soaking them is much healthier.

Soak beans overnight before cooking them, about 12 hours.

*Navy beans are an excellent source of protein, fiber, vitamins and minerals. They are great for vegetarians because of the iron content in them. Iron is an important trace mineral needed for healthy red blood cells.

Quinoa Pecan Burgers
Servings 7 patties

"Anyone can love you when the sun is shining... but in the STORMS is where you'll learn who truly cares about you!"
~Unknown

1 cup cooked quinoa

4 slices of gluten free bread toasted, use the Vitamix® blender (dry container) to make bread crumbs

1/2 cup pecans grind into the Vitamix blender (dry container) to make a powder

1/2 cup cashews grind into the Vitamix blender (dry container) to make a powder

1/3 cup unsweetened plain almond milk

2 tbsp Bragg's liquid seasoning

1/2 cup finely chopped celery

1 onion finely chopped

2 green onions chopped finely

1/2 cup mushrooms chopped finely (optional)

3 garlic cloves chopped

2 tbsp fresh chopped parsley

1 tbsp virgin coconut oil or grapeseed oil

2 tsp arrowroot starch flour (Bob's red mill) mixed with 3 tbsp warm water or 1 egg white (optional)

Sauté onions, celery, green onions, garlic and parsley, set aside.

Toast bread and put into the Vitamix blender (dry blender) to make bread crumbs.

Mix in a bowl bread crumbs, pecans, cashews, almond milk and Bragg's and sauté veggies.

Add arrowroot powder mixture or (1 organic egg white) and stir well.

Form into patties.

On Medium heat add in coconut oil and pan fry patties on both sides (about 3 min on each side.)

Put in oven for 35-40 min at 350

I love it with vegenaise, arugula and avocado on a gluten free bun.

*Pecans are enriches with many health benefiting nutrients, minerals, vitamins that are essential for optimum health.

They also are rich in monounsaturated fatty acids.

Make sure to store pecans and cashews in the freezer or refrigerator.

Black Bean Sweet Potato Burgers
Servings 5 patties

"I've learned what matters. It took a serious illness for me to learn it. But I learned it, and I'll never be the same."
~Unknown

- 2 cups organic black beans (or organic canned, BPA free)
- 1/2 cup cooked quinoa
- 1/2 cup gluten free bread crumbs or (toast 2 pieces, put into the Vitamix® blender (dry container) and grind into bread crumbs)
- 1/4 cup almond flour
- 1/2 tsp Himalayan sea salt
- 1/2 tsp cumin
- 2 tsp organic chili powder
- 1/2 tsp smoked paprika
- 3 garlic cloves, chopped
- 1 small onion finely chopped
- 1/4 cup chopped parsley
- 1 sweet potato cooked and mashed
- 1 tsp virgin coconut oil
- 1/2 cup fresh mango salsa

Sauté onions, garlic, parsley and spices in coconut oil.

In a large bowl mash the beans and cooked sweet potato. Combine cooked quinoa, bread crumbs and sautéed onions.

Mix everything all together with your hands until it's evenly mixed.

Form into patties.

On medium heat, pan fry patties with coconut oil for 5 minutes on both sides, till golden brown.

Toast some gluten free buns and top one side with mango salsa. Spread vegenaise on the other side of bun. Add arugula, avocado, and cilantro.

*Black beans are very high in fiber, folate, protein and antioxidants, along with lots of vitamins and minerals. They make a complete protein when put with brown rice or quinoa.

Amazing Beet Salad
SERVINGS 4-5

"I cannot always control what goes on outside, but I can always control what goes on inside." ~Wayne Dyer

2 cups navy beans soaked overnight or canned (BPA free) navy beans

1 small red cabbage shredded

5 cooked beets shredded

4 carrots shredded

3 cups of spring mix salad

1 cup spinach

1/4 cup red onion chopped finely

1/2 cup pumpkin seeds

1/2 cup sunflower seeds

3 avocado's chopped (make sure to put in salad at the end, so it doesn't brown)

My Yummy Dressing:

1/4 cup apple cider vinegar

1/2 cup vegenaise grapeseed oil mayonnaise (found at a health food store)

2 tbsp raw honey

1 tbsp wasabi (I buy fresh wasabi from a Japanese restaurant)

1/2 tsp smoked paprika

1/2 tsp Himalayan sea salt

Drain and rinse beans. Add beans to a large pot with 2 times the amount of water to beans. Boil for a few minutes, then cover with lid and simmer on low for 1 1/2 hours.

Boil beets till cooked, drain and place in cold water for 10 minutes.

Shred the beets using the salad master or a food processor or grater.

In a large salad bowl add all of the above and toss.

Put all the salad dressing ingredients in blender and blend till creamy.

Pour salad dressing all over and chopped avocado and toss well.

*Vegenaise tastes better than regular mayonnaise and has no animal protein or cholesterol.

Health food stores carry about 4 different types. Be sure to look for "soya free and Canola oil free."

*Beets contain fiber, magnesium, calcium, iron and phosphorus, vitamin A, C and niacin. They also contain folic acid which is necessary for the production and maintenance of new cells.

Never Ending Salad....
Servings 4-5

"Life is a gift, never take it for granted." ~Sasha Azevedo

4 cups of spring mix lettuce

1 cup of arugula lettuce

1 cup strawberries sliced

1 cup blueberries

1/2 cup of papaya chopped

1/2 cup cucumber chopped

1 orange bell pepper chopped

1/2 cup unsweetened cranberries

1/4 cup pitted chopped dates

1 red apple chopped

1/4 cup red onion chopped finely

1/2 cup caramelized pecans (see below)

1 tbsp virgin coconut oil

2 tbsp "grade 3" maple syrup

Dressing:

1/4 cup "grade 3" maple syrup

1/4 aged balsamic vinegar

3 tbsp Dijon mustard

3/4 cup cold pressed olive oil

2 cloves garlic

1/2 tsp Himalayan sea salt

In a frying pan, melt coconut oil, add 1/2 cup pecans and maple syrup, stir constantly on medium heat till the pecans become caramelized.

Blend in a magic bullet blender, balsamic vinegar, Dijon, maple syrup, garlic, sea salt and olive oil till creamy.

In a large salad bowl combine all ingredients together and toss well. Add avocado last.

I sometimes sprinkle organic goat cheese on top.

*Cranberries are packed with vitamin C to help protect your immune system. They contain powerful antioxidants that prevent certain bacteria from sticking to the urinary tract.

Kale Salad
Servings 4

"Don't start your day with the broken pieces of yesterday. Every morning we wake up is the first day of the rest of our life." ~Unknown

2 large bunches of kale washed and stem remove, make into bite size

1/4 cup red onion chopped finely

1 package small cherry tomatoes sliced

2 cups celery chopped

1 orange pepper chopped

1 avocado chopped

1/2 cup pumpkin seeds

1/2 cup sunflower seeds

1/4 cup sesame seeds

Dressing:

1/2 cup Udo's oil (or flax oil)

2 tbsp Bragg's seasoning

1/4 cup apple cider vinegar

2 tbsp freshly squeezed lemon juice

Put all liquid mixture into a magic bullet blender and blend till creamy.

Put washed kale into salad spinner to remove excess water.

Put all ingredients in large salad bowl and toss dressing really well. Top with chopped avocado last.

*Udo's oil is a blend of Omega 3 6 9 Essential fatty acids, our bodies must have them to survive, but cannot synthesize them from any other substance we eat, so a direct food source is required.

Curried Chickpea Salad
SERVINGS 4-5

"Natural forces within us are the true Healers of disease."
~Hippocrates

- 4 cups of chickpeas (soaked overnight)
- 1 red pepper diced finely
- 1 orange pepper diced finely
- 5 green onions diced finely (use all the green parts to)
- 1 cup canned watercress chopped
- 1 cup frozen organic peas (thawed)
- 1 bunch of spinach washed
- 2 tbsp raw honey
- 1/2 cup vegenaise
- 1 tbsp curry powder
- 3 tbsp freshly squeezed lemon juice
- 1/2 cup cilantro chopped

Wash spinach and set aside in refrigerator.

In a bowl mix honey, vegenaise, curry powder, sea salt and lemon till creamy.

Add in chickpeas, peppers, green onion, watercress, cilantro and peas, stir well.

Refrigerate for an hour before serving.

Place washed spinach on the bottom of salad bowls and spoon chickpea mixture on top.

Garnish with cilantro.

*Green peas are one of the most nutritious leguminous vegetables, rich in health benefiting phytonutrients, minerals, vitamins and antioxidants.

Apple Cider Salad Dressing
SERVINGS 1 CUP

"God grant me the serenity to accept the things I cannot change, courage to change the things I can, and the wisdom to know the difference." ~Reinhold Niebuhr

- 1/2 cup cold pressed extra-virgin olive oil
- 1/4 cup apple cider vinegar
- 1/4 cup water (alkaline)
- 2 organic garlic cloves
- 1 tbsp raw honey
- 1 1/2 tsp Dijon mustard
- 1 tsp onion powder
- 3 tbsp hemp seeds (found at a health food store)
- 1/2 tsp Himalayan sea salt

Blend all ingredients in a magic bullet blender. The dressing can be stored in the fridge for several days.

I like using the magic bullet blender for simple and quick salad dressings.

*Bragg's apple cider vinegar is one of my favorites! Only raw organic apple cider vinegar has the "mother of vinegar" that makes the vinegar so beneficial.

"The mother" is made up of living nutrients and has anti-fungal properties which help to neutralize fungal over growths and bad bacteria and increase the 'good bacteria.'

It is loaded in potassium which will help to eliminate toxic waste from the body.

Aioli Pine Nut Dip
Servings 1 cup

"I really regret eating healthy today...Said, no one."
~Unknown

- 1/2 cup pine nuts (soak for 1 hour)
- 1/2 cup macadamia nuts (do not soak)
- 4 tbsp cold pressed extra-virgin olive oil
- 3 tbsp freshly squeezed lemon juice
- 1 tsp Dijon mustard
- 1 clove garlic
- 2 tbsp capers (drained)
- 1 tbsp water
- 1/4 tsp Himalayan sea salt

Put all ingredients into the Vitamix® blender and blend till creamy.

Serve with homemade yam fries or on your vegan burgers.

Make sure to store your nuts in the refrigerator or freezer.

*Macadamia nuts are packed with numerous health-benefiting nutrients, minerals, antioxidants and vitamins which are important for optimum health and wellness.

Pistachio Pesto Sauce
Servings 1 cup

"You simply will not be the same person two months from now after consciously giving thanks each day for the abundance that exists in your life. And you will have set in motion an ancient spiritual law: the more you have and are grateful for, the more will be given you." ~Sarah Ban Breathnach

- 1/2 cup pine nuts (soaked for 1 hour)
- 1/2 cup pistachios, shelled
- 1/4 cup navy beans
- 3 tbsp cold pressed extra- virgin olive oil
- 2 garlic cloves
- 2 tbsp freshly squeezed lemon juice
- 2 tbsp nutritional yeast
- 1 1/2 cups stemmed basil leaves
- 1/2 tsp Himalayan sea salt
- 2 tbsp water

Add all ingredients into the Vitamix® blender. Blend on medium speed. Using a spatula, take any mixture off of the sides and blend again till everything is chopped and mixed well.

Store in a glass jar and refrigerate.

*Pine nuts have health promoting phytochemicals, vitamins, antioxidants and minerals.

Cilantro Dressing Marinade
Servings 4

"I instantly replace toxic thoughts with nurturing ones."
~Unknown

- **1 freshly squeezed lime**
- **1 tbsp sesame oil or cold pressed olive oil**
- **3 tbsp "grade 3" maple syrup**
- **2 tbsp fresh ginger grated**
- **1 tbsp Bragg's seasoning**
- **1/2 cup cilantro**
- **1 garlic clove**

Put all ingredients in a magic bullet blender and blend for about 15 seconds.

Marinade wild salmon or organic chicken, (which my family eats.)

Bake in oven for 25 min.

Drizzle left over sauce when ready to serve.

This is a marinade that is delicious and has so many flavors. On Occasion I will eat a small piece of white fish or wild Alaskan salmon. I do not support any factory-farmed fish! Be sure to check out this free documentary on line called, salmon confidential by, "Dr. Joseph Mercola."

It is a must see for anyone who consumes farmed or even wild salmon. It's an eye-opener!

*Because of the high mercury levels in fish, be sure to take chlorella. I chose to take it every day.

Hemp Hummus
SERVINGS 1 CUP

"Every cell in your body is eavesdropping on your thoughts."
~Deepak Chopra

- **1 cup cooked garbanzo beans (soaked overnight)**
- **2 tbsp hemp seeds (found at a health food store)**
- **1 tbsp sesame tahini nut butter (found at most grocery stores)**
- **1/4 cup Udo's oil or flax oil (Udo's oil is found at a health food store)**
- **1/2 tsp cumin**
- **2 cloves of garlic**
- **1 lemon freshly squeezed**
- **1/2 tsp Himalayan sea salt**

Soak bean overnight for about 12 hours.

Drain then rinse well and transfer to a cooking pot, cover with water, and twice the amount of chickpeas and bring to boil.

Cover with lid and allow simmering on low heat for 1 1/2 hours.

Put all ingredients into the Vitamix® blender or food process and blend well (add in a little extra oil, if needed.)

Make sure to store your flax oil in refrigerator up to 6 weeks once opened.

Try this with my homemade coconut naan flat bread.

*Hemp seeds are one of my favorite seeds; they are high in protein and contain all nine of the essentials amino acids (like flax.)

It also contains high amounts of fatty acids, fiber, vitamin E and trace minerals.

Vegan Veggie Dip
Serving ½ cup

"Without health, life is not life; it is only a state of languor and suffering." ~Francois Rabelais

- ½ cup vegenaise (grapeseed oil) mayonnaise
- 1 tsp Dijon mustard
- 1 tbsp raw honey
- ½ tsp garlic powder
- ½ tsp curry powder

Combine all ingredients in a bowl and mix well.

Cut up your organic veggies and serve to your family. It's a great way to get your kids to eat more vegetables.

*Curry is a combination of many spices; there are dozens of health benefits that can make for a powerful health boost as well as a tasty dish.

Red Quinoa Hemp Curry Bowl
SERVINGS 4-5

"Look back and get experience! Look forward and see hope! Look around and find reality! Look within and find yourself!"
~Unknown

- **4 cups cooked red quinoa**
- **1 red pepper chopped**
- **3 large carrots sliced diagonally**
- **1 zucchini sliced diagonally**
- **1 red onion chopped**
- **6 garlic cloves chopped**
- **2 cups Bok Choy chopped**
- **3 cups of broccoli florets**
- **1 can unsweetened organic coconut milk (BPA free) "Natural value"**
- **1 tbsp sprouted chick pea miso (found at a health food store)**
- **3 tbsp nutritional yeast**
- **1 tbsp Bragg's seasoning**
- **1 tbsp curry powder**
- **3/4 cup hemp seeds (found at a health food store)**
- **2 tbsp virgin coconut oil**

Sauté on medium heat, coconut oil, onion, garlic, carrots, curry powder for 4-5 minutes. Add in remaining veggies.

Stir for 3 min and add coconut milk, Bragg's and nutritional yeast. Place lid on top and put on simmer on low for 10 min.

Hold lid tightly and pour all the coconut mixture from the pan into the Vitamixer® blender, add in hemp seeds and blend till creamy.

Spoon quinoa into serving bowls and top with coconut hemp sauce!

*Red quinoa has an earthy, strong, nutty tasting flavor. It is rich in protein and complete with all nine amino acids. It has more calcium than cow's milk.

Mexican Brown Rice Bowl
4-5 SERVINGS

"The soul always knows what to do to heal itself. The challenge is to silence the mind." ~Caroline Myss

- 4 cups cooked brown basmati rice
- 2 cups cooked black beans or (BPA free) organic canned black beans
- 2 cups cooked kidney beans or (BPA free) organic kidney beans
- 1 green pepper chopped
- 1 orange pepper chopped
- 1 red onion chopped
- 6 garlic cloves chopped
- 1 tsp green jalapeno chopped
- 1 cup frozen organic corn niblets (non GMO)
- 1 1/2 cups cilantro chopped
- 1/2 tsp chipotle chili pepper
- 1/2 tsp cumin
- 1 tsp Himalayan sea salt
- 3 avocado's mashed with a little lemon
- 4 tbsp nutritional yeast
- 1 tbsp virgin coconut oil or grapeseed oil
- 1 bag of healthy taco chips (non GMO)
- 1 jar of mango-salsa (home- made preferred)

Drain and rinse beans. Add beans in a large pot with 2 times the amount of water to beans. Boil for 4 minutes, then cover with lid and simmer for 1 1/2 hours.

Sauté all vegetables and spices with coconut oil on medium heat for 4-5 minutes. Drain cooked beans and place back in large pot. Add in 1 cup cilantro, frozen corn and sprinkle nutritional yeast on top. Stir well and put on low heat with lid for 10 minutes.

When ready to serve, top with 1/2 cup chopped cilantro.

Spoon brown rice into a dinner bowl and put beans, veggie mixture on top.

Take taco chips and place all around the bowl and top with guacamole and salsa.

My kids enjoy a little organic sour cream with it.

*Cilantro is a great way to help the body remove mercury!

Spinach Pesto Quinoa Spaghetti
SERVINGS 4-5

"Your body's ability to heal is greater than anyone has permitted you to believe." ~Unknown

- 2 boxes of quinoa spaghetti or brown rice spaghetti (found at a health food store)
- 1 red pepper chopped
- 1 red onion chopped
- 3 green onions chopped
- 5 garlic cloves chopped
- 1 bundle of asparagus chopped in small pieces
- 1 cup mushrooms chopped (optional)
- 1/4 cup pesto sauce (see my recipe)
- 2 cups washed spinach chopped
- 1 package of small cherry tomatoes sliced in half
- 1/4 cup fresh basil chopped
- 2 tsp dried basil
- 1 tbsp dried parsley
- 1 tbsp virgin coconut oil or grapeseed oil

In a large pot boil water and add spaghetti noodles. The noodles may take a little longer, be sure to stir and check on them.

Sauté onion, red pepper, green onion, mushrooms and garlic, dried basil and dried parsley with coconut oil. Leave out spinach, asparagus and cherry tomatoes. Cook for 5 minutes.

Stir in pesto sauce and turn temperature to low. Add spinach, asparagus, tomatoes and toss. Cover with lid for 10 min.

Drain and rinse noodles. Add back noodles to pot and toss in vegetables.

Garnish with chopped fresh basil on top and a pinch of Himalayan sea salt and pepper to taste.

My family enjoys cooked organic ground turkey in this dish (optional.)

*Spinach is an excellent source of alpha lipoic acid, a potent antioxidant and cancer fighter.

It is also has bone-healthy vitamin K, calcium, folate, potassium, vitamin C, B6, B1, B2 and vitamin E, copper, selenium and zinc.

It is a very potent source of chlorophyll which is quickly metabolized and used to develop new red blood cells and put out carcinogenic substances from the body.

Organic Air Popped Popcorn
SERVINGS 3-4

"You must find the place inside yourself where nothing is impossible." ~Deepak Chopra

1 cup organic popcorn

3 tbsp virgin coconut oil

4 tbsp nutritional yeast

pinch of Himalayan sea salt

Melt coconut oil while the popcorn is popping.

Pour oil on top of air popped popcorn, sprinkle on nutritional yeast and a little sea salt on each bowl.

*One of my quick and easy snacks I enjoy at night and to take with me to a movie theater!

Nutritional yeast is deactivated yeast; it is a source of protein and vitamins, especially the B-complex vitamins. It is a complete protein. It is also naturally low in fat and sodium. It is free of sugar, dairy, gluten. It has a nutty, cheesy flavor.

Brown Rice Walnut Cashew Meatballs
Servings 20 balls

"We, each of us, must be warriors in the struggle to find our inner peace." ~unknown

- 2 cups cooked brown rice
- 1/2 cup plain unsweetened almond milk
- 1/2 cup ground raw cashews
- 1 cup ground walnuts
- 1/4 cup coconut flour
- 2 cups gluten free bread crumbs
- 2 tbsp Bragg's seasoning
- 1 onion chopped finely
- 3 garlic cloves chopped
- 2 tbsp fresh parsley chopped
- 2 tsp of arrowroot starch flour (Bob's red mill) mix well with 3 tbsp warm water in a cup
- 2 tsp virgin coconut oil or grapeseed oil

Preheat oven to 350.

Sauté on medium heat coconut oil, onion, garlic, parsley till veggies are almost cooked.

Toast 4 pieces of gluten free bread and put into the Vitamix® blender dry container and grind into bread crumbs. (I use coconut bread or brown rice bread.)

Combine all ingredients, add in arrowroot mixture and form into small little balls.

Place them on a cookie sheet and bake for 40-45 minutes.

Great for Spaghetti!

Make a double batch and freeze them and warm in oven when needed.

*Raw cashews are a great source of fiber and protein; they provide heart healthy monounsaturated fats and several vitamins and minerals. They are a great source of selenium, potassium, folate, phosphorus, copper and magnesium.

Sweet Potato Burrito's
Servings 5

"I choose to make the rest of my life the BEST of my life!"
~Louise Hay

3 cups cooked brown basmati rice

2 cups of cooked mashed sweet potato's

1 19 oz canned red kidney beans (BPA free) or 2 cups of soaked overnight (cooked beans)

5 gluten free tortilla shells (if you can't find a healthy gluten free wrap, look for Ezekiel sprouted wrap)

1 green pepper chopped

1 red onion chopped

1 cup of non GMO organic sweet corn kernels (I buy frozen)

1 cup cilantro chopped

1/2 cup olives sliced

1 tbsp chili powder

1/2 tsp cumin

1/2 tsp chipotle spice

1/2 tsp Himalayan sea salt

6 garlic cloves chopped

1 freshly squeezed lime juice

1 tsp virgin coconut oil or grapeseed oil

3 avocado's mashed with a little lemon juice

Cut up sweet potato into smaller pieces and boil for 10 minutes.

Sauté onion, garlic, green pepper, cumin, chipotle spice, chili powder in coconut oil till the veggies are nearly cooked.

Put thawed corn, mashed potatoes, rinsed beans into the Vitamix blender® and blend till creamy.

Pour bean mixture into sautéed veggies.

In a bowl combine rice, lime juice, olives & cilantro.

Place all tortillas on a flat surface with lots of room to spoon both mixtures on top.

Start with bean mixture then rice.

Roll tortillas and place on a cookie sheet.

Brush olive oil on top to keep from browning too much while cooking.

Cover with foil.

Bake for 30 minute at 350.

Serve with Fresh guacamole & salsa.

My family enjoys a little bit of organic sour cream on top.

*Garlic contains hundreds of minerals and nutrients. Healing traditions have recognized garlic as a natural "wonder drug."

Now medical research indicates garlic may prevent heart disease and cancer.

Coconut Quinoa Delight
Servings 4-5

"The best way to escape from the past is not to avoid or forget it, but to accept and forgive it." ~Unknown

1 1/2 cups quinoa

2 cups organic unsweetened canned coconut milk (BPA-free) "Natural value"

1 cup of water (alkaline)

4 green onions chopped finely

2 large potatoes sliced and chopped in half

1 green pepper diced finely

4 garlic cloves chopped

2 tbsp ginger grated

1 tsp chili flakes (optional)

1 tbsp nutritional yeast

1/2 cup cilantro chopped

Freshly ground pepper to taste

Add quinoa, coconut milk, water and all the ingredients and bring to boil, put lid on and bring the temperature too low for 15-20 minutes.

Let cool for 5-10 min with lid still on.

Add pepper to taste.

This is one of my favorite dishes and it is so quick and easy to make for your family.

* Quinoa is one of the most protein-rich foods we can eat. It contains almost twice as much fiber as most other grains.

It also contains iron, lysine, magnesium, B2 and Manganese.

Brown Rice Noodle Pad Thai
SERVINGS 5

H.O.P.E. Hold on, Pain ends. ~Unknown

1 box of brown rice thick noodles (found at health food store)

1 red onion chopped

2 cup cauliflower chopped

1 cup snow peas with ends cut off

3 garlic cloves

2 carrots thinly sliced diagonally

2 cups broccoli florets

3 green onions thinly sliced

1/2 cup cilantro chopped

3 baby ' heads' of baby Bok Choy chopped

2 tbsp Thai kitchen red curry paste "clean ingredients" (found at grocery store)

1 tbsp virgin coconut oil

2 tbsp Bragg's seasoning

1 tbsp sesame oil

1 tbsp raw honey

2 tbsp cashew butter

2 freshly squeezed lime juice

1/4 cup organic unsalted peanuts chopped (optional) or raw cashews chopped

In a large pot boil water add noodles. They may take a little longer than white noodles.

Drain and rinse noodles and lightly drizzle 1 tsp of olive oil and toss.

On medium heat sauté onions, garlic, coconut oil. Add in cauliflower, broccoli, carrots, snow peas and Bok Choy with coconut oil on low-medium heat for 5 minutes and stir well.

Combine in a bowl, Bragg's, red curry paste, honey, lime juice, sesame oil, and cashew butter.

Pour sautéed vegetables and curry paste mixture in with noodles and stir well.

Sprinkle peanuts on top.

*Broccoli is one of the richest sources of iron in the vegetable world. It's high in levels of vitamin C, beta carotene, and fiber. Broccoli is a powerful antioxidant that helps to prevent damage to cells caused by free radicals, believed to be a factor in cancers.

Pesto Pizza
Servings 4-5

"Strength does not come from winning. Your struggles develop your strengths. When you go through hardships and decide not to surrender, that is strength." ~Mahatma Gandhi

- **4 gluten free pizza shells (found at a health food store)**
- **1/2 cup pesto sauce (see my recipe)**
- **1/2 cup organic pizza sauce**
- **1 green pepper sliced finely**
- **1 red pepper sliced finely**
- **3/4 cup red onion sliced finely**
- **1 cup mushrooms sliced finely**
- **1/2 cup olives sliced**
- **Sprinkle goat cheese on top (optional)**

Bake at 350 for 25 minutes

Let cool for 10 minutes before serving.

My family enjoys organic ground turkey on top. (Sauté ground turkey with 3 tbsp of pizza sauce.)

*Ergothioneine is an antioxidant which is in mushrooms; it is powerful for the immune system. Selenium and vitamin E work together to protect healthy cells from damaging effects of free radicals we are bombarded every day with.

Cheesy Brussels Sprouts
SERVINGS 5

"True courage is to keep on traveling when you can't see the map." ~Unknown

- **6 cups Brussels sprouts**
- **1/4 cup sliced almonds**
- **2 tbsp virgin coconut oil**
- **3 tbsp nutritional yeast**
- **2 garlic cloves minced**
- **Pinch of Himalayan sea salt**
- **Freshly ground pepper**

Wash and cut ends off the bottom.

In a large pot bring to boil, cover and steam for approx. 10 min on medium heat.

(I like to leave them a bit more on the crunchy side.)

Drain and set aside in strainer. Add coconut oil to the pot and pressed garlic cloves, stir for a couple min on medium heat.

Turn off heat, add nutritional yeast and sprinkle a few toasted almonds on top and a pinch of Himalayan sea salt and pepper to taste and stir well.

This is one of my Favorites!

*Plant phytonutrients found in Brussels sprouts boost the body's natural defense systems to protect against cancer and other diseases.

Brussels sprouts can help your body eliminate bad Estrogen."

Vegan Nut Cheese
SERVINGS 1 CUP

"Life is an echo... what you send out comes back. What you sow, you reap. What you give, you get. What you see in others exists in you." ~Zig Ziglar

- **1/2 cup raw almonds (soaked overnight)**
- **1/2 cup raw sunflower seeds (soaked overnight)**
- **1 tbsp dried dill or 2 tbsp fresh dill chopped**
- **1 small garlic clove**
- **1 tbsp red onion freeze-dried flakes**
- **2 tsp nutritional yeast**
- **3 tbsp fresh lemon juice**
- **1 tbsp apple cider vinegar**
- **3 tbsp water**
- **1 tbsp cold pressed olive oil**
- **1 tsp sprouted chick pea miso (found at a health food store)**

Soak nuts with twice the amount of water as beans overnight in a glass bowl.

Drain and rinse well. Add all ingredients into the Vitamix® blender and blend well.

The sides may stick to blender, take a spatula and take off sides and add a little extra water.

Store the nut cheese in a glass jar in the fridge. It will last several days.

I enjoy this delicious cheese with gluten free crackers or a cream cheese spread for a sandwich.

*Make sure to buy organic nuts, almonds easily absorb pesticides because of their high oil content.

*Almonds are one of the most nutritious of all nuts. They are low in saturated fat and contain calcium, magnesium, vitamin E and compounds called, phytochemicals which may help protect against cancer.

Honey Mustard Kale Chips
Servings 3

"Do not go where the path may lead, go instead where there is no path and leave a trail..." ~Ralph Waldo

- **2 large bundles of kale**
- **½ cup raw cashews (soaked for 2-3 hours)**
- **1 tbsp Dijon mustard**
- **2 tbsp raw honey**
- **2 tsp Bragg's seasoning**
- **2 tbsp cold pressed olive oil**
- **1 tbsp apple cider vinegar**
- **2 tbsp nutritional yeast**
- **2 tbsp hemp seeds (found at a health food store)**

Preheat oven to 180 degrees.

Wash and stem kale and put into salad spinner. Make sure the kale is really dry. Place the kale pieces on some paper towel and leave it on the counter to dry while your cashews are soaking. In the meantime I like to prepare my sauce. In a pot melt honey, Bragg's, olive oil, apple cider vinegar, and nutritional yeast, mustard and hemp seeds. (Do not boil.) Stir until creamy. Drain cashews and add them into the Vitamix® blender along with the melted mixture and blend until creamy. When ready to make the kale chips, add dried kale into a large bowl and pour the blended mixture all over the kale. Using your hands toss really well, making sure every piece is coated.

Place the kale on top of a large roasting tray, which has holes. That way the air can circulate and get them crispy. Place the tray at the bottom of the oven rack.

Bake for about 2 ½ hours.

Enjoy! These are a healthy and delicious snack for you and your family.

*In order to reap the benefits of honey, we must only consume honey that is raw or unpasteurized. Honey is loaded with many essential vitamins and minerals. It is an excellent source of antioxidants.

It supports good bacteria and has antibacterial and anti-fungal properties.

Sweet Potato Mash
Servings 4-5

What Cancer Cannot Do; "Cancer is so limited… it cannot corrode faith, It cannot shatter hope, It cannot cripple love, It cannot destroy peace, It cannot kill friendship, It cannot suppress memories, It cannot silence courage, It cannot conquer the spirit, It cannot invade the soul, It cannot steal eternal life." ~Unknown

4-5 large sweet potatoes peeled and cut into big chunks

1 tbsp virgin coconut oil

¾ cup light coconut unsweetened milk (BPA free) "Natural value"

½ tsp Himalayan sea salt

In a large pot boil water. Add sweet potatoes, boil till cooked. (Make sure to check them with a fork, and do not overcook them.) Drain and place them back into pot with coconut oil, coconut milk and sea salt.

Using an electric beater, blend for a couple minutes till creamy.

*Sweet potatoes contain almost twice as much fiber as other types of potatoes. They contain vitamin B6, potassium, vitamin A and manganese. Manganese is a trace mineral that has some great health benefits. It helps support healthy blood sugar levels, which helps stabilize the appetite for hours.

Coconut Dream Balls
Servings 15 balls

"Forgiveness is not something we do for other people; we do it for ourselves - To GET WELL and MOVE ON!"
~Unknown

1 cup of raw whole almonds

1/4 cup pistachio nuts (no shell) or raw cashews

1 cup pitted unsulfured dates (soak in warm water for 30 min, and drain)

1/3 cup raw organic unsweetened cocoa powder

3 tbsp hemp seeds (found at a health food store)

¼ cup white chia seeds (found at a health food store)

2 tbsp sesame tahini nut butter (found at most grocery stores)

1 tsp organic vanilla

2 tbsp "grade 3" maple syrup

1 tsp virgin coconut oil (melted)

3/4 cup unsweetened shredded organic coconut

Put almonds into the Vitamix® blender using the dry container and grind into a powder with tiny pieces of almonds. Do not over blend the almonds.

Repeat the same with the pistachio nuts.

In a bowl combine almonds, pistachios, hemp seeds, chia seeds and cocoa powder.

Add soaked dates, maple syrup, coconut oil, tahini, vanilla into the Vitamix blender and blend until very creamy.

Pour liquid in with dry ingredients and stir well. (I like to use my hands to mix.) The mixture should be sticky and hold together.

Spread the shredded coconut on a large plate.

With clean, wet hands, roll the mixture into 1 1/2 inch balls. Roll them in the coconut till fully covered.

Store them in a container in the fridge.

*Unsulfured dates contain no additives. Dates are rich in minerals like iron and B vitamins and vitamin C. They contain soluble and insoluble fibers and different kinds of amino acids. Dates are extremely low in calories.

Organic Peanut Butter Cookies
Servings 20

"If you don't take care of your body, where are you going to live?" ~Yobi Yamada

- 1/2 cup coconut flour
- 1/2 cup all-purpose gluten free (Bob's red mill flour)
- 1/2 cup sorghum (Bob's red mill flour)
- 1/2 tsp arrowroot starch flour (Bob's red mill)
- 1/2 tsp baking soda (non-aluminum)
- 1/2 cup "grade 3" maple syrup
- 1/3 cup virgin coconut oil (melted)
- 1 tsp vanilla
- 1 cup organic crunchy peanut butter or pecan butter
- 1/4 cup cacao nibs
- 1 tbsp organic cocoa powder
- 1/4 cup apple sauce

Preheat oven to 350.

In a large bowl combine all flours, baking soda, arrowroot, cocoa powder and cocoa nibs.

Put peanut butter, maple syrup, apple sauce, coconut oil and vanilla into the Vitamix® blender or food processor and blend on low till creamy.

Pour into dry mixture and mix well.

Make into balls.

Put on cookie sheet, flatten with a fork.

Bake 15 minutes.

Make sure to store your nut butters in the refrigerator.

I buy arrowhead mills crunchy "Valencia" organic peanut butter. Valencia peanuts are safe from fungus because of where they are grown in Arizona (dry, arid climate.)

*Organic raw coconut flour is high in fiber, protein and is gluten free.

Almond Butter Maple Cookies
Servings 12 cookies

"Life's challenges are not supposed to paralyze you; they're supposed to help you discover who you are." ~Bernice Johnson Reagan

- **1 cup gluten free all-purpose baking flour (Bob's red mill)**
- **1/2 tsp baking soda (Bob's red mill)**
- **1/4 tsp Himalayan sea salt**
- **1/2 cup almonds chopped**
- **1/2 cup almond butter**
- **1/4 cup "grade 3" maple syrup**
- **3 tbsp unsweetened vanilla almond milk**
- **2 tbsp coconut oil (melted)**
- **1 tsp organic vanilla extract**
- **3 unsulfured pitted dates**

Preheat oven to 350.

In a large bowl, blend together flour, baking soda, and salt.

Pour into the Vitamix® blender maple syrup, coconut oil, dates, vanilla, almond milk and blend until creamy.

Pour ingredients from blender into the bowl of almond butter and mix well.

Add dry ingredients to wet, stir until combined. Fold in almonds.

"Refrigerate dough for an hour."

Roll dough into small balls, place onto cookie sheet lined with parchment paper.

Press down with a spoon, they will look like a maple leaf! Bake for 13 minutes, until the edges begin to turn golden brown.

*Maple syrup "grade 3" is the least refined and is richer in minerals. It contains manganese, zinc, calcium, iron, potassium and magnesium.

Best Cocoa Avocado Pudding
Serving 2

"No matter who tries to teach you lessons about life, you won't understand it until, and you have to go through it on your own." ~Unknown

1 large ripe avocado, peeled and quartered

1/4 cup organic raw cocoa powder

2 tsp freshly squeezed lime juice

Pinch of Himalayan sea salt

1/4 cup "grade 3" maple syrup

1/4 cup vanilla almond milk (unsweetened)

1 tsp organic vanilla extract

unsweetened shredded coconut

Put all ingredients into the Vitamixer® blender and blend until creamy.

Garnish with fruit and unsweetened shredded coconut.

Put in the refrigerator and chill till ready to serve.

* Avocado is high in oleic acid, which has been to shown to prevent breast cancer in numerous studies.

They are also an excellent source of glutathione, an important antioxidant that researchers say is important in preventing aging, cancer and heart disease.

*Glutathione: One of the most effective ways to encourage the body to make this antioxidant is to eat avocados, asparagus, walnuts, broccoli, apples, spinach and tomatoes.

I highly recommend taking milk thistle. I take 20 drops 2x a day in my alkaline water.

Yummy Coconut Butter
Servings 3/4 cup

"We are only given TODAY and never promised TOMORROW, so make sure you tell the PEOPLE who are special in your life, that you LOVE them!" ~Unknown

- **1 bag of unsweetened shredded coconut (250 grams)**
- **3 macadamia nuts**
- **1/2 tsp organic vanilla extract**
- **1 tsp organic unsweetened cocoa powder (optional)**
- **1/2 tsp water**

Pour the bag of coconut into the Vitamix® blender on medium low.

I like to run the blender for 6 min till the coconut is ready.

The Vitamix blender will stop a few times, so take a spatula and bring the sides down and blend again. Add in 1/2 tsp water, vanilla, cocoa powder and nuts.

It may stop a few more times, and then it will get creamy. The blender may get hot after 4 minutes. Turn it off and let it cool down for 5 minutes. Then start it up again for the remaining time.

Store the butter in a small glass jar in the pantry.

Try it on my banana chia bread, oat flax pancakes, quinoa cocoa muffins and my pumpkin muffins!

*Coconut butter has amazing antifungal, antiviral and antibacterial properties. This boosts up the immune system and helps to fight off various forms of infections.

Yummy Protein bars
SERVINGS UP TO 20

"My soul honors your soul. I honor the place in you which the entire universe resides. I honor the light, love, truth, beauty and peace within you, because it is also within me. In sharing these things we are united, we are the same, we are one." ~Namaste

2 cups organic quick oats (Bob's red mill)

1/2 cup unsweetened canned coconut milk (BPA free) "Natural value"

2 tbsp raw honey

1/2 cup organic natural peanut butter

¼ cup sesame tahini nut butter (found at most grocery stores)

6 tbsp of vanilla Vega protein powder

1 tbsp golden brown flaxseeds (grind in the Vitamix® blender (dry container)

1/4 cup pumpkin seeds

1/2 cup of hempseeds (found at a health food store)

½ cup sliced almonds (for the topping)

½ cup shaved unsweetened coconut chunks (for the topping)

1 organic 85-90% dark chocolate bar (100 grams)

Mix all ingredients in a large bowl, except sliced almonds and coconut. Using your hands mix well. Add a little extra coconut milk if needed.

Line parchment paper on cookie sheet, spread out the dough onto a cookie sheet.

Melt dark chocolate in a sauce pan and spread on top. Sprinkle almonds and coconut.

Put tray in the freezer for 30 minutes.

Take out and cut into squares. (I cut mine into bigger chunks.) Store the bars in a large container in the freezer.

*Make sure to buy only BPA free canned coconut milk. My favorite brand is organic unsweetened Natural value. It is BPA free, guar gum free and is Kosher.

1 cup of unsweetened coconut milk contains 50 calories.

*Coconuts are rich in lauric acid, which is known for being antiviral, antibacterial, and antifungal and boosts the immune system.

Life IS A GIFT, I ACCEPT IT.
LIFE IS AN ADVENTURE, I DARE IT.
LIFE IS A MYSTERY, I'M UNFOLDING IT.
LIFE IS A PUZZLE, I'M SOLVING IT.
LIFE IS A GAME, I PLAY IT.
LIFE CAN BE A STRUGGLE, I'M FACING IT.
LIFE IS BEAUTY, I PRAISE IT.
LIFE IS AN OPPORTUNITY, I TOOK IT.
LIFE IS MY MISSION, I'M FULFILLING IT.

Made in the USA
Charleston, SC
27 March 2014